I AM GOOD WITH ME

A compilation of inspirational messages and positive affirmations for children.

Kishma Anthony

Illustrated by Hayford Kesse

LANIER PRESS

Giving thanks to my Heavenly Father without whom none of this would be possible. To my beloved parents, Henry and Georgina Anthony. I would be remiss to not say thank you for the inimitable love, kindness, and support you have exemplified throughout the years. I am grateful to have been raised by parents who individually and collectively shaped the ways in which I view myself and ultimately the world. . . whether I am accepted or not because I am *indeed,* Good With Me. *And as the late author Maya Angelou states, "I sustain myself with the love of family."*

Kishie

LANIER PRESS an Imprint of BookLogix
Alpharetta, GA

ISBN: 978-1-6653-0204-3 - Paperback
ISBN: 978-1-6653-0205-0 - Hardcover

Library of Congress Control Number: 2021915701

Printed in the United States of America 082721

♾ This paper meets the requirements of ANSI/NISO Z39.48-1992 (Permanence of Paper)

Cover and illustration by Hayford Kesse. Author photo by Cherise Richards.

For ordering information, visit KishmaAnthony.com.

Author's Note to Parents:

If there is one piece of advice I learned from my mother as a child, and it still resonates with me to this day is to . . . "Choose People Who Choose You."

And if I am being honest, I really didn't fully grasp the magnitude of the message she was trying to convey until I got much older.

It's one of the reasons I wrote *I Am Good With Me*. I think it is critical that children learn who they are as individuals, and are aware of the wonderful qualities and value they add to life.

It is what helps them to discern that they are not necessarily for everyone, and everyone is not for them.

It is what helps them to be confident enough to walk away when they are not accepted or respected by others.

It is what helps them to not force what does not fit, and to question who they are if it doesn't.

So I urge you to make a concerted effort to inspire, uplift and motivate your little ones . . . they are listening.

Do you know that being comfortable with who you are as an individual is a very important part of growing up? When you feel good about yourself, you are confident enough to try new things and are proud of your gifts and abilities . . . even when you make mistakes.

We all experience shyness and having doubt. Even adults too! But you should never let that get in your way. The goal is to always strive to be yourself, and it doesn't matter what anyone says or thinks because you are unique and special. And as silly and simple as it may sound . . . being good with yourself is quite fun!

So . . . why are you good with you? Let's look at the reasons why you should be comfortable with yourself.

I am good with me because I was created with purpose and I am **AMAZING**!

I am good with me because I'm strong and can achieve anything I set my mind to.

I am good with me because I am loved and I love who I am.

I am good with me because
I'm happy being me.

I am good with me because I'm silly.

I am good with me because I'm smart.

I am good with me because I’m intelligent.

I am good with me because I'm confident.

I am good with me because I'm a leader.

I am good with me because I'm fearless.

I am good with me because I'm brave.

I am good with me because I'm creative.

I am good with me because I'm positive, and being positive inspires others.

I am good with me because I'm caring.

I am good with me because I'm friendly.

I am good with me because
I am going places.

I am good with being all of the wonderful things that make me great at being **ME** ... because I am proud of who I am becoming.

Okay, great! So with that being said, at the count of three let's shout it out really *loud* ... strong and **PROUD**!

I ... AM ... GOOD ... WITH ... ME!

The End

Discussion Questions

1. What makes you happy?

2. What are some things that you like about yourself?

3. What would you like to be when you grow up?

4. What do you enjoy doing?

5. What does it mean to be confident?

About the Author

Kishma Anthony is an enthusiastic, creative, and inspirational individual. Her books highlight her quest to ensure children grow into happy, healthy, thriving adults who chase their dreams and aspirations.

Other Books by Kishma Anthony

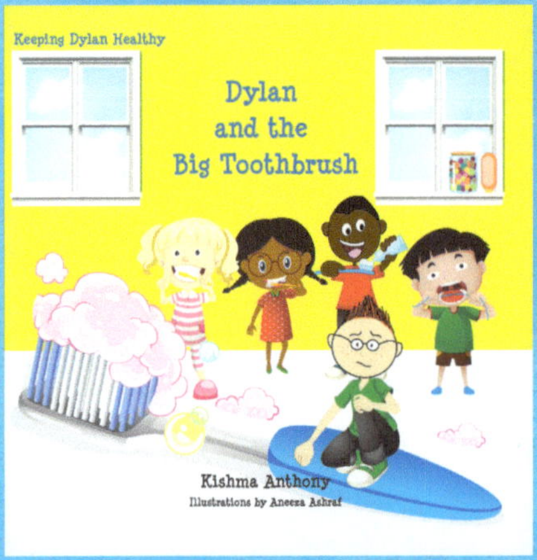

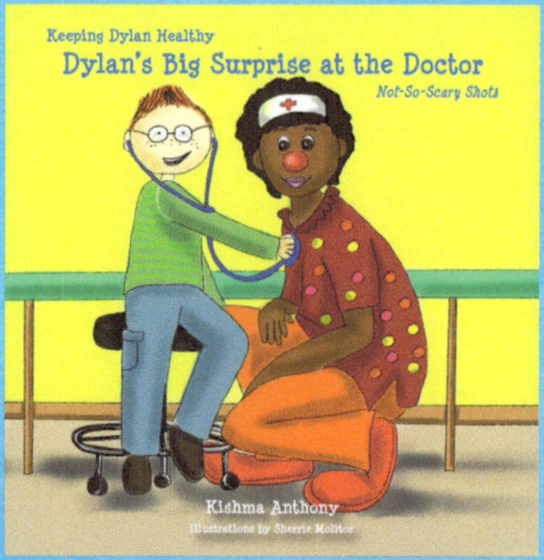

www.ingramcontent.com/pod-product-compliance
Ingram Content Group UK Ltd.
Pitfield, Milton Keynes, MK11 3LW, UK
UKHW061030310726
14089UKWH00009B/176

* 9 7 8 1 6 6 5 3 0 2 0 5 0 *